THERE WAS FIRE IN VANCOUVER

Sinéad Morrissey

THERE WAS FIRE IN VANCOUVER

CARCANET

First published in 1996 by
Carcanet Press Limited
402-406 Corn Exchange Buildings
Manchester M4 3BY

A CIP catalogue record for this book
is available from the British Library
ISBN 1 85754 230 4

The publisher acknowledges financial assistance
from the Arts Council of England

Set in 11pt Palatino by Bryan Williamson, Frome
Printed and bound in England by SRP Ltd, Exeter

for Conor

Acknowledgements

Acknowledgements are due to the editors of the following publications, in which some of these poems have previously appeared: *Atlanta Review, College Green, The Cúirt Journal, Icarus, Ireland's Women: Writings Past and Present* (Gill & Macmillan/Kyle Cathie, 1994), *PN Review, Poetry Ireland Review, Religion & Literature* (Indiana).

Contents

Double Vision

Friday. Eight o'clock. Pissing rain.
Belfast a shallow bowl of light,
The Black Hill a power failure
Touching the sky.
I've seen it all. But the places in your head
Stay shut to me, and I'm grasping at why.

You've travelled up as I have,
Shifted home for the odd weekend,
Same road, same car, same weather –
But the world could be under water
With me none the wiser.
None of what I saw is in there.

You saw somewhere gone into, somewhere gone.
Elsewhere, you wish.
The REDUCE SPEED NOW sign
A red flag in your face
And every street lamp a chorus in neon: *You're Back* –
Glimmering with victory.

Among Communists

I remember smoke and faces that I knew
And the fact that I got in free; my mother
Taking money by the half-collapsed sink;
Posters proclaiming 'AN EVENING OF BRECHT'
And subtitled: *Bring Your Own Drink;*
Too much conviction to see through.

CND

I want to grow up, not blow up! –
My slogan balloon and my CND badge
And my grin on the front of the *Belfast Telegraph*.
Nine years old and filled to the brim
With my parents' demands for peace.

The Trade Union Congress on Fallout
Stretched through Saturday.
Between a windowless Bangor and a melting city
I signed hate mail to Reagan,
Collected stickers, tasted beer.

It wasn't until I saw two skeletons,
Scared of the sky, of the hole in the high-rise,
That it began to mean tears.
The still fear of being nothing too soon and too suddenly
Silenced me for the day.

Ciara

We wandered in one Christmas afternoon
On our way to the lakes to ask for her company,
But she was crying over potatoes.
My parents stayed with her till they took her away.
There would be no walk.

I noticed a fishtank, her old blue slippers,
The bewildered mother and the silent child,
Formed an image in my head of boiling potatoes
And wondered about their powers of catastrophe.

Then, bored, I walked the outside wall,
Under the beginnings of stars,
Until a white van pulled in along the gutter.
She was shuttered off from view.
Ruined Christmas.

The potatoes stuck in my mind.
Something easier for her to articulate
Than the mess of love and various motherhood,
Than the son who had his knees blown somewhere else.

A frightening rain, pouring out
Of the Armagh sky, had filled the lives
Of Ciara's household. One shattered woman
A fraying edge of the legacy.

Eleven

They rolled stones in Connemara
Down the sides of hills.
Two pairs of boots and the laughter of boys
Dancing round the top of the sky.

Their laughter was malice.
I saw their imaginations pinned on me
And felt myself selected for harm.
Their aim was simply to displace the mountain.

Rocks and men were gathering time,
Slicing my way to the holiday cottage.
When the sun went down, it went down out of shame.
It stayed down for four years.

A Performance

This garden is so empty of time it holds me still, unable to go on.
I blame the leaves: they fell from the sky in such a wild, golden rain
They pulled me in, to see them thigh-deep over flowers and graves
That had been stamped with names and dates, faith and pain,
Like flags on sinking ships. No more years to go by, all whos
And wheres washed out in nature's fire, the only death here
Is Autumn's, and she does it too well. The trees' bold undoing
Is no serious grief, but an accomplishment of practice.
I wonder what faces the graves will have
When Winter is here, and her show is over.

Saturday

Noon. I stand
Behind net curtains,
Watch kids on the street
Throwing stones.

Buses pass each way.
An ambulance,
In all its slowed-
Down urgency, forces through.

His heart must have stopped
Between the newspaper
And a glance
At the races. Something

Lurking
That caught up with a shock
And sucked him
Out of all he knew.

Europa Hotel

It's a hard truth to have to take in the face –
You wake up one morning with your windows
Round your ankles and your forehead billowing smoke;
Your view impaired for another fortnight
Of the green hills they shatter you for.

Belfast Storm

With a rain like that lashing into the city
And a wind that blew streets dark before you could blink –
It's as though the angels are angry, sitting in the sky
With heads in hands and howling it out all over us.

I can't think what they haven't got used to by now.
The great gap in the street where his knees hit the wall
Meant wheelchairs, rather than coffins.

English Lesson

Today I taught the Germans about Northern Ireland.
High on their interest, I paraded as a gunman
On the Falls Road. Death holds the attention –
BANG! blew them off their seats and I got away scot free.

'A fiddler in a death-camp' –
Beyond the lot of it.

The only honesty is silence.

Thoughts in a Black Taxi

1

Four days to go until the twelfth, and the bonfire is fourteen feet high.
I want the driver to drive ten times around the diamond.
I've been gone too long –
I want to stare and stare.

I imagine winding my way through the *Dump Wood Here* signs
And the fallout of black tyres,
Dismantled shelving and donated sofas
To the bare-chested men swanking about on top.

Fascinated by the organisation,
I want to ask them where they got their ladders from.
One 'What are *You* called?' from them, and it would all go black.
I'd have to run to stay whole.

2

It's not as though I haven't blundered before –
Asking what UYM means by the Rushpark estate,
Or laughing at how the Germans think Paisley is mad
In a taxi heading east of the city.

I never registered thrown looks for hours afterwards.
My father sweated.
Even ordering I get it wrong these days –
This rank is UVF-run. Never say Morrissey again.

3

My teeth were so crooked it took six months at the Royal Victoria
Before I could smile without denting my lower lip.
Six years of the Grosvenor Road in a state high school uniform
Was like having *Protestant* slapped across your back.

I always walked with my heart constricting,
Half-expecting bottles, in sudden shards
Of West Belfast sunshine,
To dance about my head.

In the Valley of Lazarus

There are ten of them I know, men who sit sullen
Over coffee and schnapps in their huts on the cheeks
Of the mountain. Some fell as far as fifty metres,
Limping back later with rods and tape
To gauge the distance of their miracle.
Others aimed too suddenly at the sun
On motorbikes, Toyota vans, a borrowed BMW or a forester's tractor –
Then crashed like stars into darkness.

One lost his looks but wore his scars as medals.
Another swore, as the trees
Avalanched in his head,
He heard voices, and built gnomes about his house
As big as tables. Each of them came back.
All countries discovered,
There was no shocking them.

That Summer

There were two deaths that summer,
And they entered my world second-hand
From the realm of the stranger. One of them died
Without knowledge of the grief that cried
Out at her: her ultimate demand
To be understood, now inarticulate forever.

There was little chance for bravery,
Perhaps no time for shame.
For she died shot down from her starting flight
Of life: the room of herself still empty of light,
The door still shut. The other died in pain,
Searing and forewarned, yet he did so in a glory

That she had not been granted.
For, knowing the future, he opened like a flower
In the crude face of death. He strained to reach God,
Across the barriers stained with his blood,
And the face of death became that of a lover.
He died completed, whilst she died stranded.

Let me not think only of her life clubbed
Out in a backstreet, of her unheard crying.
For her death could sour forgiveness
With such an image of its own violence.
Instead, let me also remember my lost cousin dying,
Who left peace in my world, if not love.

Bosnia

He went up like a Roman candle and shocked all the wrong people.
The emotional ones, who thought it meant giving a damn,
Cried into their breakfasts. And then whatever light
His singed features sparked off in the world went out.

A short circuit overloading on murder reports and war,
He ignited in open air, his own apotheosis. He knew
They wouldn't stop him, burning fingers and faces; that they'd allow
His flame of protest to dance on the Westminster lawn.

The World is Not Round

Beyond the West Coast
There is no Pacific, no Japan
And no globe to suggest
A continuous journey –

There is only the precipice
One hundred miles down
Piling up with apartment blocks,
Bullets and drugs –

The Fall that the sailors
Failed to feel
As Columbus set faith
On the skyline

There Was Fire in Vancouver

There was fire in Vancouver,
And we leaned out into the night to watch it
Set light to the East End.
It had taken stand on Commercial Avenue.

We marvelled at the darkness of the city,
All neon dulled by the superior flame,
And wondered would it bestow its dance
On the Ginseng Teahouse in Chinatown, on Jericho Pier.

There were no sirens, hoses, buckets even,
Scattering streets and 'Fire!' 'Fire!'
We seemed the only ones concious of the bright crusade
And we watched with Moses standing in our heads.

You

for D.W.

Never looked me in the eye for weeks on end,
Or if you did, I was elsewhere
And you did it sideways. We were
Two fast crabs digging into the sand.

Now there are no holds barred. Painfully,
Sometimes. The urgency you need to defy
Modesty! Meanwhile I've slipped out with the tide,
Astonished at how I return such scrutiny.

Love Song

I see light everywhere
Over the bus driver the woman
With her trolley in the street
I see dusk

I hear the clock at four
I hear silence in cupboards
Birdsong
Backwater dawn

I taste drier than flour

I smell the roots of trees
Before I see their arms
Shrieking
On the skyline

I feel diamonds pushed into
The bloodstream
Self-generated, a gift,
Making for the head I feel my head

Thrust into
A bucketful of stars
And all my senses
Singing

Clothes

Once they come undone, there's no stopping the undoing
Of all that keeps us us and not we.
From a room full of history and underwear
I throw out my diary and walk naked.

Until we're talking of weather again,
Contact shrunk back to wherever it sprang from.
And I'm begging for it all, coat, hat, gloves, scarf –
Shoes shod in iron, and a waterproof.

The Mirror on the Ceiling

I took it down two years ago, but he still comes knocking.
There was too much space in him.
I gave him everything on the outside –
The long curve of my spine; arms, feet, thighs.
He was the actor and director of his own imagination,
Dying for every exterior. The moving
Crown of my head was the rising star in his heaven.

Never whole and never alone, I got to wanting it
Without sight of it. No show, no reflection –
Not even in his eyes, which were so outside of himself,
So beside himself, so down on every last cell of himself –
I craved for nothing but blind discretion.
He stands on my doorstep, pleading his lost barbiturate,
But the mirror is in the outhouse. I promise cobwebs, whitewash.

The Fort-Maker

It was too late for invasion
By the time he'd set his hungry eye on the hill
Above the town, and thought of the view.
War was not the reason
For the three years' haulage –
It was sheer love.

And because his need
Was a beginning and an end to all things,
His house became a circle of windows –
Catching ruins and birds
And the blank faces of the sea
In a stilled frame, everywhere he looked.

A Week of Rain

for Síle O'Sullivan

And most of us are so under the weather
It takes two days of sunshine to dry out our blues.
You've been glued to the window in your room.

The falling, by breaking silence, brings it home.
You're rapt in the peace of it, remembering winters
In all those secluded Big Houses in Ireland

You grew up in and lorded over.
When it rained then, the whole world contracted
To the sounds of footsteps and silk.

A Visitor

The bathroom smelled of lemons and the surfaces shone –
I thought she'd worked to make me feel welcome,
But things were just too well placed.
Everything screamed her in her own absence. I felt ousted.

Scared of neutrality, she'd rubbed herself into wood
Until it shone her own smile; put postcards in corners,
All with a history, and that deep red everywhere –
She wore it always.

I couldn't stand her nudity
In the endless smiles of pre-Raphaelite women,
Balanced over rivers, singing dirges.
I knew they'd drown in flowers helplessly

And that helplessness burned me in those rooms of hers,
Her fear of existence not being her own
Like grafitti on walls *I am here I am here* –
I could go nowhere.

She squashed her kindness out.
I left the keys next door and a note that my mother
Was sick in Derry, thanking her anyway.
I shook her grief from my shoes as I stepped outside.

Mercury

1

BOTTOM DRAWER

Her bottom drawer lay filled with all her life:
Diaries and letters and photographs and gifts.
A testimony to every rage and every kiss
And every moment when the light gave shape
To that precise outline of who she was:
What stars were hers, what frosts.

Intricate as a snowflake, intact as childhood,
No gaps where fear had burned the evidence;
No sudden invasions, or abandoned residence,
Or loss. She had it all by heart, document by document,
And kept it locked. A Chinese vase being painted in
By time, beautiful and brittle as bone.

2

NOMAD

It's this leaving of villages,
One after the other –
The repeated conclusion
It's not here either –
Beauty, home, whatever –
That leaves you where you are,
Where you always are –
Side-stepping yourself, side-
Stepping the days you find no sense in,
And facing the road.

From scarecrows to gantries,
A skyline of signatures,
Cranes that defy
The skies they're built in.
And cities,
And the back ends
Of cities. No place to walk through,
No space to hold. Your books and your spoons
In a walled up room,
Somewhere you can't get back to.

GULL SONG

Thunderstorms do nothing I shelter
In my own wings fly over the torn monastery
And the open altars of the land and come clear.
I have nothing to fear in weather or distance –
It is my heart pumping out
Its own crumpled urges –
The music of my loneliness
That I cannot fly free from.

4

FINDING MY FEET

Today I found my feet and vowed
Not to let them leave again.
I dived into the sea to save one:
He found the coral more interesting
Than the sky and answered the only journeys
Are inward. But the lack of oxygen
Had turned him grey, and I dragged him to air.

The other was holidaying in Bangladesh,
In raptures with the stars and how far he'd made it,
In danger of making it the whole way round
And running out of room to run away in.
I flew him home first class. They kicked at first,
But I built them a room with underwater lighting
And a door, making them stay.

5

LEAVING FLENSBURG

This city settled on you in layers of days
That brought a grounding with them, that sense of knowing
Where your feet belonged. Memory built the way
In which you recognised the place, decided how much your going
Would cost: a few confused days in the next stop-over, or dreamscape
     for a year.

This one was a hard one to guess, because although
Your feet knew all the town's directions,
And tapped their way through the map they'd got to know,
They never saw their own reflection
In the Baltic harbour: the thousand jellyfish that swarm in in September

Made the glass shiver and the sky disappear.
All the same, you had the Glucksburg Autumn, days when the gold
Set loose in the sky seemed almost like a crime. You feared
The winter, but it came, and the darkness and cold
Brought with them skies of stars, high over Schleswig-Holstein, singing
     in space.

Above all, the shipyard rocketed the price –
Freezing and full of sad men welding steel. It was almost dark
As the finished freighter slid out to the sea, and the thin ice
Cracked in the shapes of flowers, all the way to Denmark.
It was then you knew there'd be dreams for years.

6

NO NEED TO TRAVEL

The tulips are nodding their heads in the garden,
Six bright faces in a grey spring rain,
Holding court to your stories of Africa –
The time, the plains, the colours the rains bring

And I think how something of the nobility
Of the wilderness broke ground here also
In that knack of knowing how to thrust colour skywards,
Flaunting the unlikely, shocking through bloom.

Hazel Goodwin Morrissey Brown

I salvaged one photograph from the general clear-out, plucked
(Somehow still dripping) from the river of my childhood.
You in your GDR-Worker phase, salient, rehabilitated:
Reagan, you can't have your Banana Republic and eat it!
Your protest banner and your scraped back hair withstood the flood.
I've hung your smile beside your latest business card: *Nuskin Products*.

Contact address: Titirangi, New Zealand. Out there a psychic
Explained how, in a previous life, I'd been *your* mother,
Guillotined during the French Revolution. You were my albino son.
You saw fire in the windows. This time round we returned to the
    garrison –
Swanned round Paris in the summer playing guess-your-lover.
I wonder how many of our holidays have closed down cycles.

Anyway, I believe it. Because when you drove to the airport
And didn't come back, it was déjà vu. And I had to fight,
As all mothers do, to let you go. Our lived-in space
Became a house of cards, and there was nothing left to do but race
For solid ground. You settled your feathers after the flight
In a fairytale rainforest. Discovered the freedom of the last resort.

Glaciers

There is no sea in my blood.
There is nothing that cannot be stopped.

God's wand is absolute.
Looking at glaciers

Jinxed into stillness –
I miss oceans in my head.

Awaiting Burial

Being born was as painful as this –
The crusade of the heart to bloom in mist,

The pull of blood
On everything the body had

To pump in a new direction,
The sliding dissection

Of water
And air –

Getting the heart to falter
And the lungs to breathe water

Requires
The tonweight of the sky,

A damaged hillside, night-time,
The tunnel you dreamt of, O

Sarah, speak to me, you've been through
The journey, was there light on the other side

My Grandmother through Glass

*Birth and death are doors: you go out through one
And come back in through the other.*
                                        – Hugo Gloor.

I

Your mother, perhaps, will greet you now,
Or the spirit-children you never had
Whose faces pushed against that line for years.
Hoping. Misting the glass. Dying to be born.

You said you felt the weight of their plea
As eyes on your back in an empty room
Or a flock of pestering voices beyond your range.
Their whispering nagged your mind.

Then his pit accident, your hysterectomy
Or the usual, age-old seep of indifference
Stopped intercourse for good.
After that, those tiny moon-faces were crushed.

II

The one who broke rank, the one
With the mastered knack of negotiating glass
As you just turned twenty-two,
You bedded down in the three-roomed house

On Bamford Street, and called Rosemary.
Your sister-in-law, Sarah, who knew all the herbs,
Insisted. *There's Rosemary; that's for remembrance;*
Pray you; love, remember –

III

My Great Aunt Sarah was the daughter of a gypsy
And on her way out when my mother was born.
You said she loved your husband as her own.
She laid out the dead, delivered

The furious children, buried
Two sisters who were rotten with anthrax,
And never married.
Love poems to Grandfather

Were found in a drawer two days after
The stroke that killed her. Her World War I
Boyfriend had drowned in a submarine that lost
Its way back to the light.

IV

My mother never forgot her gypsy blood
And broke rank all her life.
At four she caught cabbage butterflies
On her own, at fifteen was gone

For weeks, and three months after
You buried your husband
You heard she wasn't coming home.
Two years later she sailed in for a visit with a screaming boy and girl.

V

Sarah helped with the delivery
From the other side. Dead a virgin,
She'd seen enough of childbirth to know
How the tunnel of pain can terrify

And sent my mother sleep in labour, an afternoon
Of April rain, sagaciousness.
When she woke from her dreaming she just wanted to push.
The nurses wept with laughter

As I entered the world with a shower of blood.
Sarah saw me off with a message of love –
To give you all the kindness she never could. She said
Jealousy over her brother's body had closed her throat.

VI

You've gone through the glass and into the arms
Of the children who cried to break into your body.
Your mother will be young again.
No negotiation from this side in –

The glass descended and shimmered open
And then froze hard again beyond all normal view.
No doubt your own face changed.
No doubt memory followed you.

VII

And me? I'll stand in your empty house
And regret my message.
Grown tall among my childhood photographs
Framed by your bed

And the stopped clock,
I'll rage at such an absence.
At what the sky stole.
And even the knowledge that sometime, way back,

Both of us were moon-eyed children
Who played together in the land of glass
Won't kill the awful hush of your departure
Or stop the flesh constricting in my heart.

Losing a Diary

I

Semi-ship-wrecked in the harbour at Howth,
The fishing trawler (or cargo boat,
Or one man's lifelong retirement dream proved excessive,
Washed up and rusted) skulked in the sun.
The radio was on in the bridge but no one listened.
Tied down to everything it was and wasn't,
The whole crate bobbed and creaked. On the prow
Stood a two-litre carton of milk, sliced
Neatly in half, and full of old rain water.

II

Losing a diary is losing a line to the harbour.
I enter the past in open sea, leave in storm
And none of what I visit can be moored or married
To the sad, fixed honesty of how it was.

To Look Out Once from High Windows

Cost you your railway lines, washing lines, sex on billboards
Seven feet high, pissing in gardens, smoking in bedsits, dust.
Cost you the choice you never made so you could be lost
In the closest way to being found: the quicksand of a wife, in-laws,
The decrease that children bring, or an attic full of yourself only
Only yourself and only as you tell it – wanking and lonely.

Underneath your choice lay the surest way of being found:
To pass all the marriages, births, and seaside hols by
On an express train through life that doesn't stop. It was the honesty
Of death you wanted. Its silence was stunning, like the white surround
Of an all-round prison wall. The way life broke down to enter it was
    what
You couldn't bear, making young girls' summer photographs so falsely
    stopped

And irretrievable. To look out once from High Windows was to fly
Over the walls you saw in life, in life's renunciation
And beyond, and to accept that endlessness might mean resolution.
All words broke there. You stopped your various desolations colliding
By just looking up. You built your runway out of decimated love
And saw in flight how nothing could be left to lose or prove.

After the Hurricane

You saw the wind as the breath of God.
You couldn't help it. Your refusal of the ether
That would mist over death got smashed to splinters
Like the Florida coastline, up-ended in rain.
There was too much rage in the sky for it not to be God's.

Perhaps it was your position under the window,
At the mercy of whatever startled missile
Made its appearance next –
A tree, a house, a woman –
Over your head. You saw a shower of cars

Spat out like sycamore seeds
And a landscape that trailed wires
In its rush to be pure.
You felt too temporary not to be answerable
To the power in the break up of hills.

September Light

There won't be light like this for another year.
It's value is the four weeks it exists in, rareness making gold.
The skies of the city hold it well, jutting out chimneys
Like broad thumbs to the sun to bear witness before it falls.
I thank God that days like this are numbered.

Twenty-One

I don't know why God gave the world,
But I am in it. Looking up, I want to photograph
The blown blossom and the receding colours of the day –
To affirm my sky as beautifully as a blackbird.

Guardians

Light is their element, they make waves
In the world with the force of their rays.
They are close by in this valley,
Swept in with the rain and snows of winter.
They hover but have no wings.
They cast shadows in their brightness,
Letting us know they are here. They exist
In the sudden illumination of our days and bear love,
Making sure the earth holds as we climb the last mountain
And come out at the plateau before cities grew tall
And where minerals dazzle.

My New Angels

God's old angels made us peaceful.
They had wings of love and explanation.
They brought us our destiny to lower our eyes
And let everything be for a reason.
There was no bewildering them.

My new angels are howling, hard,
And there are masses in heaven
For every snuffed out light on a back road.
Their rage is assured, ragged, unforgiving.
There is no perfecting them.

Her Love

Something fell on her in childhood –
Her father's disapproval, the sky –
Something obdurate. She's stumbled blind
Round the landscape of her own head
Ever since, halved by the impact, and six inches high.

She gives herself away on doorsteps, in alleyways,
Bedrooms she sees once only,
For neither love, nor money.
The men are all faceless, she never asks them to stay –
She is trying to get tall, she is singing her injury.

What use is my wringing of hands?
The tears I send her as showers of rain?
She locks me into a cold house with her denial
Of God. At the end of my outcry she still stubbornly stands
Where escape is a brick wall, and all angels are lame.

Our Utmost

I murdered once in life. Don't ask me how I deal with this here –
Her mouth in mid-scream, some withering death-mask,
Sewed stiff with catgut to my own. He was severe.
He told me: *The stitches will release themselves with grace,*
It is grace alone. Teach them grace and grace shall set you free.
So I sought you out. I am that voice you seek to smother
When the rage descends and you grasp for weapons.
If you listen once, you'll keep your face free
In the shadows here, and I'll be given back my own
From under the leaves and buried treasure of her smile.

If Words

If words became things
I'd watch a stream of unfortunates
Fall from the mouth –

Harlequin, leather,
Worn shoes and a megaphone
Blasting the second-hand
Book of the self; animal masks,
Nitrate, and all the small-minded
Weapons of fear – double-edged
Penknives, the hypodermic,
The wasp –

They spill like sewage and dismay.
I dream of the mouth as a nest
Giving flight to

Lilies, windows,
Gold letters and chimes,
Witch-hazel, a lighthouse,
An oak beam, a warm sea
And a bright white body
In the act
Of forgetting itself –
Shuddering with love.

The Juggler

He must have practised for hours
Between the bins and the mattresses
Of a rented back yard
To dance the seven painted skittles
Off his fingers like that.
He has the game whittled

To art. God knows what
Anachronism he took up before,
Using medieval skills to stop
Time: he puts the clock back
Nine hundred years
With this side-show for a quack

Or diversion for a king.
Still, or because of the drain
Of things modern, we ring
Him with faces. He knows
How we anticipate failure
And that what he owes

His audience is a defiance
Of breakdown. We watch as his magic
Creates the radiance
Of a spinning blue arc, brought
Slowly to standstill. Natural begrudgers,
We are nevertheless caught

By the weightlessness, the controlled
Mechanics of air

With all the improbables cajoled
Into truth, we are not as far out
From faith as we were.

Monteverdi Vespers

for John McManus

The voices sing me to a dark room, with a wall
Three parts window and a grey sky. Outside
There's a terrace where gulls have stalled
On the eggbox chimney-pots. I hear them cry.

I know the knacks of gulls: after rain how
They stamp the lawns to fool the worms.
I know they fly to chimneys to be warm, cower
Nowhere, fought shell to be here, stern

As the shark and its off-shore wreckage,
Where I've heard they hover. *Jerusalem,*
The voices sing. City compacted in faith and damage,
The cry of gulls accompanies you with knowledge.

Wish

I'll stand you by the Mourne Wall
And it shall be Easter. Sheep and mist
And a wind that would blow you to Ballynahinch.

I hang on your every word,
But the wind is too greedy, and as curious as I am.
I have to catch them in flight before they cartwheel down the valley:

Jesus Cold Viking Afterworld

And I would become a tent for all the winds of this gully
To keep them off you. Then, blown huge but still
In range, I would hear again your vision of hills.

Restoration

1. ACHILL, 1985.

Once I saw a washed up dolphin
That stank the length of Achill Sound,
Lying on the edge of Ireland.
The Easter wind ripping it clear
Of all its history,
And the one gull watching it,
Abandoned by the tide.
I remember how its body,
Opened in the sun,
Caught me,
And I remember how the sea
Looked wide and emptied of love.

2. JUIST, 1991.

The North Sea booms tonight
And there are no lights the length
Of the fifteen mile beach,
And no stars

The sea is revealing itself
By its own light light revealing
Essences of light:
Meeresleuchten, lights of the sea

One touch and the water explodes
In phosphorescence
No one knows if it lives
It is as though God said

Let there be light in this world
Of nothing let it come from
Nothing let it speak nothing
Let it go everywhere